W9-CMP-690

(previous pages)

The Lamar River flows
north, then westward,
off the shoulder of the
Absaroka Mountains into
the Yellowstone River.
On this quiet June evening I waited in
my favorite part of Yellowstone for the
moon to rise above Saddle Mountain.
Two days before the moon would be
full, there was still sunset light on the
land as the moon rose above the hori-
zon. Vegetation was in its peak growth,
the river was falling after the spring
floods, there were uncounted thousands
of new animals in the valley, and the
moon's soft round light shone on this
paradise. I call this a perfect spring day.

THE LIGHT *of* SPRING

THE SEASONS OF YELLOWSTONE

by Tom Murphy

Crystal Creek Press

The Light of Spring is the first of a four-volume set by Tom Murphy called *The Seasons of Yellowstone.* The turning of a full year in Yellowstone Park gives us four distinct seasons. Each one overlaps and flows into the next one but has its own unique character.

Spring's uniqueness comes from the powerful pulse of light warming the land. It starts and maintains the growth of vegetation and supports the birth of a myriad of creatures.

Summer is defined by the growth of the wildlife and the luxuriant leaves, flowers, grasses, and forbs. The long warm days and cool nights make it the most pleasant and easy season.

Autumn brings maturation and independence for the young animals, the rut and mating season for many large mammals, and the drive to put on fat for the coming winter. It is the time for the seeding of plants and starting the process of dormancy for trees, bushes, grasses, and forbs.

In winter the struggle to endure and survive the harshest weather of the year is evident in every part of Yellowstone. It is the season of simple, quiet, clean beauty. Snow sweeps over the landscape reforming the land into smoother and softer shapes while the cold, at the same time, is brittle and sharp.

Please send us your name and address if you would like to be notified when future volumes are released.

All photographs in this book are available as archival giclée prints.

Crystal Creek Press, 402 South 5th Street, Livingston MT 59047 406 222 2302

Copyright © 2004 by Tom Murphy
Second Printing 2007
Published in 2004 by Crystal Creek Press
Livingston, Montana

All rights reserved. No portion of this book may be reproduced, stored in a retrieval system, or transmitted in any form or by any means without the prior permission of the publisher.

Book design by Adrienne Pollard
Printed and bound in China by C & C Offset Printing Co., Ltd.

ISBN 0-9668619-1-4 (clothbound)

Yellowstone's spring can look like winter, spring, or summer.

Winter is still very evident in late March. I have skied across Yellowstone in March in twenty below zero F temperatures. In early spring the snow begins to settle and melt. As the snow banks shrink they are dirty, because the pine needles, dust, lichens, and other embedded materials that fell and blew around over the snow become visible on the surface. April is referred to as mud month, when the snow recedes and exposes long-buried brittle vegetation, pocket gopher trails, and soil churned up by the runoff.

Ungulates at the beginning of spring are at their weakest, thinnest, and most fragile. Depending on the weather, late winter or early spring is often the highest period of winter kill. The fat reserves, which carried the animals through the cold snowy winter, have been depleted. They may not have enough strength left in early spring to survive if the melt-off and warmth do not give them relief soon. Even the ones who survive do not look great. In the spring warmth they shed their sun-bleached winter hair in patches and remind me of Salvation Army thrift store couches.

Many animals emerge in spring from hibernation, all of them hungry. Ground

squirrels often appear on the top of the snow looking for fresh green vegetation in the blinding bright light after six months in total darkness.

The rebirth on the landscape is the most spectacular aspect of spring. The extended daylight, the rapid growth of vegetation, the new green, and the wild array of flowers give us a rebirth of our own spirit. All births are tied to the explosion of other births, the wild growth of plants, and the abundance of insects. A few birds, such as owls, nest in late winter so their young hatch at the same time that young rodents begin to appear above ground in April and May. One of the icons of Yellowstone, the bison, begins its birth cycle about the 20th of April and continues for a month. The rest of the ungulates begin their birth cycles about the 20th of May and also continue for a month.

During this two month period, when shivering little newborns are on the ground, it could be a sunny 70 degrees F or it could be 20 degrees F with three feet of wet snow. With each birth, a newborn's struggling, bewildered, innocent energy mimics what went before but carries the possibility of new strengths. The mother's amazement and tender nuzzling has much of the same innocence and optimism as the struggles of the newborn. They hold the future there for themselves, for us, and for all of life in the universe. I see how small and fragile each of us is, yet how over-whelmingly powerful the force of life is.

Migratory birds return optimistically to raise another generation in a place that has been uninhabitable to them for the past six or seven months. The spring season floods warmth, light, and food over the land to provide the nursery for uncountable animals from mosquitoes to grizzly bears. Birds move through this world utilizing nearly every niche, some are feeding on stone flies under the water in Slough Creek, and some are feeding on the spiraling clouds of midges in the Hayden Valley. Birds observe Yellowstone from all kinds of places: the broad soaring wings of a red-tail hawk from 1000 feet above the Lamar Valley, a group of cowbirds from the fuzzy back of a bison, or the dipper from its wet mossy nest stuck to the misty cliff alongside Tower Fall.

A plant gets help dispersing its offspring by producing edible fruit, berries, and seeds. But flowers: what a clever way for a plant to recruit insects, birds, and bats to partici-pate in its reproduction. The most creative, selfish, and devious thing a plant does is to produce flowers with aromas, colors, and shapes which attract an entirely different kingdom of creatures into its parlor. It could be inviting catastrophe, but by giving an animal a bit of sweets, a root bound plant gets clever, active creatures to carry its genes to the handsome neighboring plant three feet or three miles away. The animal thinks it is stealing nectar, but the nectar was actually just the bait. The plan all along was to have a wild excess of pollen and sweets laid over the path or flung over the bodies of the welcomed thieves and passively let them go on their way to steal other's nectar. Scuffling crea-tures unintentionally carry pollens to all the parlors they visit, much to the plant's benefit and the animal's total ignorance.

There is a steady succession of color and variety in Yellowstone's flowers. The earliest spring flowers, such as dogtooth violet, springbeauty, fritillary, and shooting star, give way to the ones that wait until the ground is warmer: fairy slipper, geranium, blue flax, and silky phacelia. The colors are scattered, mixed, pooled, and clustered on the land. One week, a meadow will exhibit a light rosy haze from thousands of shoot-ing stars; then a few weeks later the domi-nant color is yellow from cinquefoil and buttercup, then even later, the blue of wild iris. The colors of spring change in one area as the season progresses, but the colors also move up the mountains because an increase in elevation works like an increase in latitude. Early spring vegetation appears along the lower Gardner River in April but doesn't arrive at Dunraven Pass until June. We can have all the colors of two seasons somewhere in Yellowstone through most of June; and when it is summer around Gardiner, it is early spring on the Absaroka and Gallatin Divides.

In my photographs, I try to illustrate in a simple, relevant, and clear way the beauty of our natural world. We can see only what we understand; therefore, one role of art is to expand our circle of awareness. The complex natural world will forever keep us straining to gaze out beyond the present reach of our awareness. Each of us came from the same star dust, yet we often make our individual uniqueness a barrier to other life. Every other life has the same individual uniqueness as ours, visible if we look closely. As we travel on our short visit here we constantly commingle with other parts of the universe. We share the water, the air, and the soil with all other creatures. Starlight touches us from suns faded to darkness long before our sun appeared. These particles of matter that we now call ours came from stars and will eventually become parts of other stars. To positively influence our world, we must carry our unique and communal star dust so that we contribute light and beauty to this space and this time we have. —TM

A robin chose to nest inside a tree that had been burned by the fires of 1988. She had used dull, dead grasses and a tree charred a velvety black to build a cradle for her delicate eggs. These four eggs, colored like the sky, held a hope of new life in an expanse of completed lives.

Douglas fir

Mountain bluebirds are
one of Yellowstone's first
returning migrant birds.

They start to appear in March. Their bright
blue plumage stands out in sharp contrast
to the snow and dull brown vegetation that
prevails in early spring. This male perched
on the top of a small lodgepole pine,
watching for insects in the early grasses.
It was snowing lightly and the cold damp
breeze caused both of us to fluff up and
try to stay warm.

Gardner Canyon and McMinn Bench

Grizzly bear, May snowstorm

During an early June snowstorm these two bull moose moved across Blacktail Plateau.

They had survived the past long winter in good health and were starting to grow their new antlers for the year. I watched them briefly in the heavy wet snow, big flakes smacking into my left ear. The snow muffled every other noise. Even the giant feet of these moose made no sound in the dead grasses and sticks.

Hayden Valley,
June snowstorm

From Artist Point, there is
a magnificent view of
Yellowstone's Grand Canyon.
Remnants of the previous winter's ice and
snow clung to the canyon walls. Winter
was trying to extend its time with a hazy
snow shower, obscuring the low ridges
in the distance. I was far enough away so
the falls, and even the river below me,
were quiet; the soft haze of falling snow
reduced the vastness of Yellowstone to a
more intimate scale.

Brown headed cowbirds
are insectivores, and they
are often seen walking
and fluttering around
the noses and feet of
grazing ungulates.
Localized disturbance by an elk or bison
grazing in a clump of grass causes the insects
to panic and scatter, creating an opportunity
for the cowbirds to find and catch them.
A huge, warm bison back is also very
attractive as a perch and sometimes as a
meeting place for the whole flock.

The blue grouse is one of two gallinaceous or chicken-like birds native to Yellowstone.

The male's early spring courtship behavior includes prancing around with his tail fanned out, his wings drooping at his sides, and red tympanic membranes inflated and exposed on his neck. A deep humming, gulping sound, along with the visual display attracts the female. If the hen likes what she sees, she will allow the male to approach her. This male grouse was displaying on the ground for a hen who was perched about 30 feet above him in an aspen tree. The hen and I observed his efforts as he strutted back and forth in the grass. Nearby, a large fallen aspen tree was tilted at about a 35-degree angle. Deciding that it was a good stage for his performance, the male strutted over to the lower end of the log and hopped up on it. It had been raining for the past several days and things were still wet. The hen and I watched as he grandly began strutting up the log in full beautiful display. The bark was gone from the log, so the gray, wet surface was especially slippery. He made it about two yards up the log, then both of his feet flipped up in the air, and he disappeared in the rose bushes below. All the hen and I could see were the tops of the bushes wiggling around as he struggled to get out into the grass again. She looked down at the twitching rose bushes, then over at me, and back to the bushes. About a minute later she flew away. The male finally struggled out from the bushes, wet, bedraggled, and in disarray. He looked up to where the hen had been and, after a brief pause, walked back into the bushes.

Green lichens on rotten log

Morning light,
Mount Everts

The largest waterfowl in North America, the trumpeter swan is also the most majestic and graceful.

It once was common, but due to hunting and habitat destruction, it was regionally almost extinct by the 1930's. Yellowstone is now home to about 40 individuals with about 1000 visiting in the winter. The orange on their heads and necks is a mineral stain from iron oxides in Yellowstone's water and mud which they have picked up while dipping their heads underwater to feed.

Trumpeter swan
cygnet

Tower Fall

Raindrops on false solomon seal

The Yellowstone Plateau is a significant part of the backbone of North America.

It holds some of the headwaters of three of the United States' major rivers: the Columbia, the Missouri, and the Yellowstone. Uncounted thousands of cold and hot springs, hundreds of waterfalls, and hundreds of small unnamed feeder streams splash, tumble, and roar down through Yellowstone. The spring floods from snow melt and cold rains create a soggy landscape, perfect for a nursery that surges to life with the warming sun.

Lying on the edge of the ice rimming the Lamar River, this adult otter was trying to eat her fish.

Her two pups beside her thought they deserved part of the fish. She held the fish out over the moving water to prevent thievery, frustrating the pups. It was now early spring, and the pups were big enough to catch their own meals. The only piece the pups eventually got was the trout's head, after mom dropped it and swam upstream.

Sunrise over fog, Hayden Valley

In a light rain this coyote was hunting one afternoon in early April. I watched her for several hours while she searched for rodents along the barely greening meadows on the north side of the Madison River....

She had caught only one meadow vole in those two hours, which is poor hunting. There were a few ground squirrels in the area, but they were very wary and dove into their holes before the coyote could get anywhere near them. The need to get something to eat was pushing both the coyote and the ground squirrels to be out on the ground.

I watched the coyote tense up, lower her body, and face intently off to my left. I looked ahead of the coyote and was surprised to see a ground squirrel sitting at the mouth of its hole about 15 yards in front of the coyote. All the rest of the ground squirrels had immediately dropped down their holes and disappeared before the coyote was even 30 yards away. Staying

crouched down, the coyote began to carefully walk directly toward the ground squirrel. The coyote moved her feet in a smooth fluid way so there was no sudden movement, not even one toe out of line. The squirrel didn't move. It seemed to be mesmerized by the way the coyote floated slowly toward it. The coyote stopped about ten feet away and, with very little external

sign, tensed up her muscles and felt for a good stance to launch herself forward. I think the coyote was watching the ground squirrel's body language, waiting for a little relaxation of its concentration; because when she made her dash, the squirrel was delayed just a little before it dropped down into its hole. The coyote made two long leaps and was at the hole with the squirrel

going out of sight. For an instant, I thought the coyote had missed, but she had caught the rear legs of the squirrel, and as her momentum carried her past the hole, she spun around and pulled the squirrel back up out of its refuge. The coyote shook its prey sharply and bit down hard because the squirrel was biting the coyote's cheek. The coyote shook the squirrel hard a

couple of times and dropped it. She picked it up immediately, bit hard and dropped it right away so the squirrel wouldn't have a chance to bite her face again. When the squirrel was dead, she ate it, head first. In less than 15 seconds, it was gone. She licked her lips, sniffed at the empty hole, and walked off to find another meal.

Swan Lake Flat after sunset

Thunderstorms are one of my favorite weather events.
The air is cool, agitated, and alive;
suddenly there is an intense flash of light....

Depending on the distance to the lightning bolt, a crack, boom, or rumble usually follows. Lightning activity is most active near the leading edge of a storm front. If the storm cell is moving relatively slowly,

I set up a tripod in the dark, and using a wide angle lens, attempt to catch the flashes of light while the shutter is open. Most of my lightning images are at least several minutes long. Luck is always a

large part of the success of lightning photographs because there is no way to predict exactly where the bolt will be and no time to move and compose when it does flash.

Gang of bull elk in velvet

Elk, moose, caribou, and deer make up the deer family, and only they grow antlers.

Every other mammal with hard pointed projections growing out of its head has horns. Antlers are made of a bone-like material and are grown and shed annually. While a bull elk's antlers are growing from April to August, they are covered with a soft, brown fuzz called velvet and are blood-rich, warm, and relatively fragile.

Geysers are one of
nature's rarest and most
intriguing phenomena.

They exist only in young volcanic rock.
Over half of all the geysers in the world
are in Yellowstone Park, and they are as
beautiful as waterfalls. Actually, they are
exceptional waterfalls; they have one wild,
furious current surging upward fighting
gravity. At their heights the sparkling
columns of hot water hang for an instant
in the cool air at the peak of their erup-
tions and then collapse back to the ground
like normal waterfalls, surrounded by
soft billowing steam.

Evening sunlight on hills,
Lamar Valley

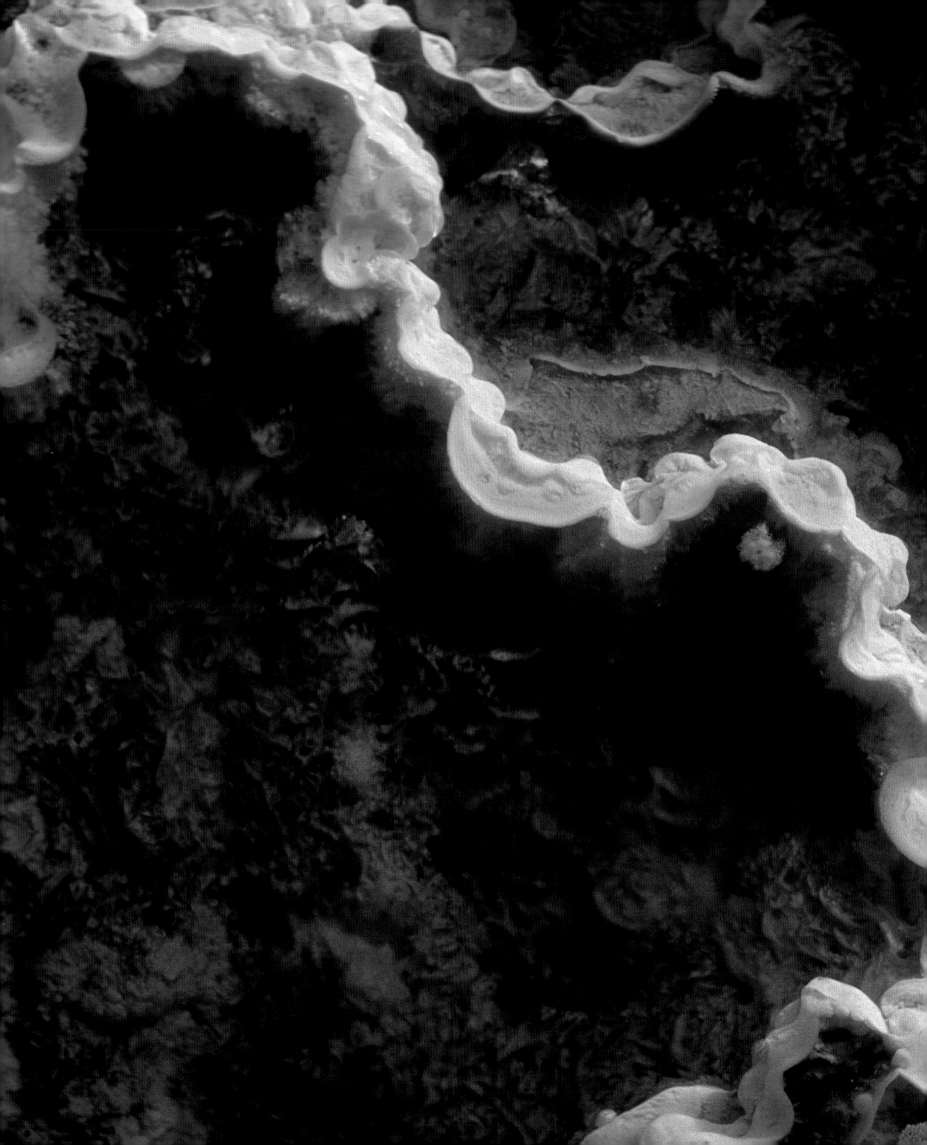

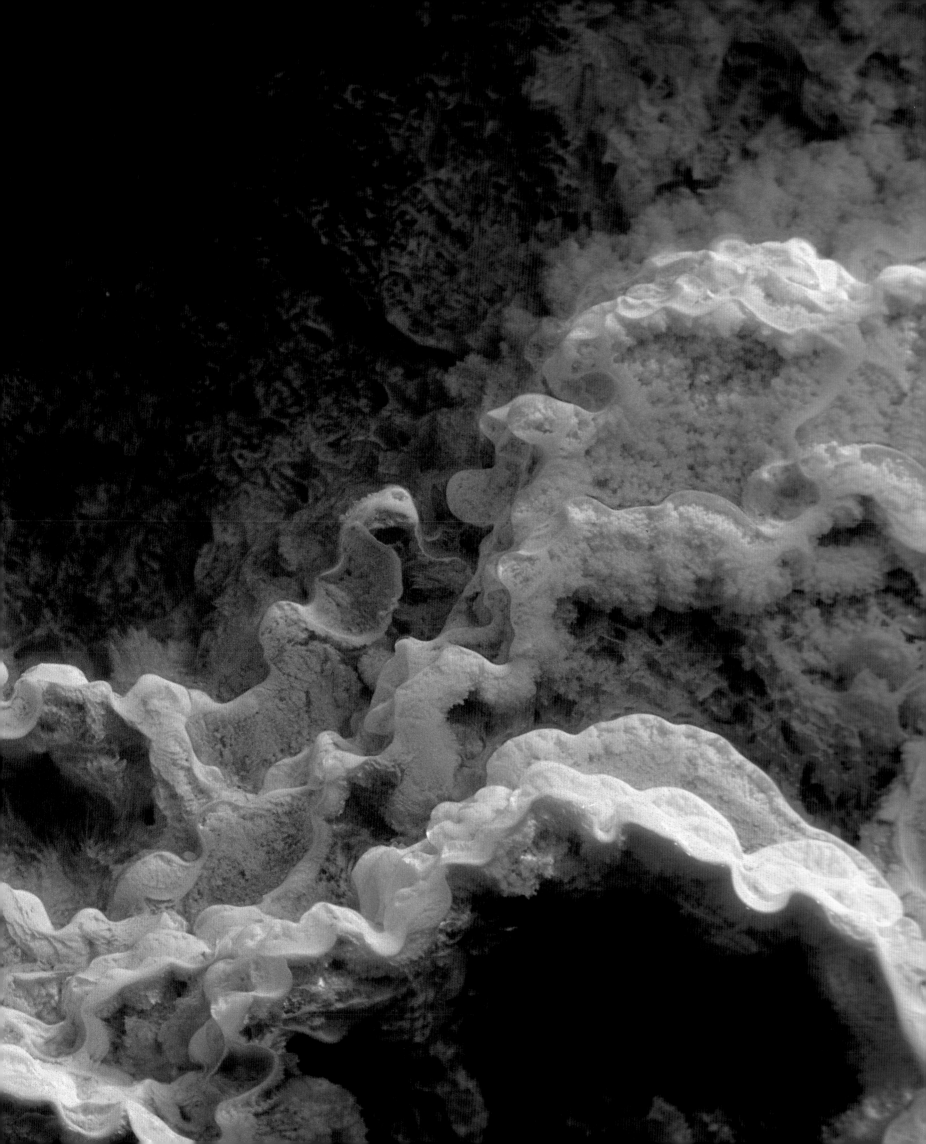

Sunrise sunstar through fog in cottonwood, Lamar Valley

(previous pages)
Travertine lace detail,
Mammoth

The songs of many birds we describe as joyful.

By saying this, we anthropomorphize their behavior, because many bird songs are apparently just individuals yelling about their claim to a piece of territory. House wrens, such as this one on Swan Lake Flat, sing joyfully in the early morning sun. He sang a varied, liquid melody in the clear cool air for almost 15 minutes. The many musical phrases he sang were repeated eventually, in different sequences, which made the song complex and captivating.

Slough Creek below Cutoff Mountain

Cutthroat trout spawn in the spring in shallow, clear, cold mountain streams.

This stream was about 18 inches deep. By setting the camera on the bottom of the creek with the lens pointed downstream and using a 12 foot cable release, I was able to photograph the trout while crouching on the bank. This was a great opportunity to see how fish maneuver gracefully in an environment so foreign to a non-swimmer like me. The name for a group of trout, a "hover" of trout, makes perfect sense from this angle.

American white pelican swimming
with mergansers

Cliff swallows nest in colonies.

To build a nest they collect mouthfuls of
mud from the edges of puddles and streams.
Carrying the mud to a vertical surface,
they spit out each little blob and construct
a hollow hemisphere about the size of a fist
with a 1-1/2 inch diameter entrance tube
pointing out and slightly down. They
produce a weatherproof nest lined with
feathers and soft grass with a lumpy mud
stucco exterior. This is a bird so agile it has
no predators while in flight. It is quite a
contrast for it to sit quietly in the dark
interior of a hard little shell glued to a wall
during the nesting season.

A scientific explanation of how the iron compounds in rhyolite

are chemically altered by hot water
doesn't explain why the soft pastel colors
in the highly eroded canyon walls are
so beautiful. This much color in a large
landscape is impressive and unusual.
Most Yellowstone landscapes have
more vegetation obscuring the ground.
Here is a rare opportunity to see the
surface structure of a very large
erosion feature.

Lower Falls under
rising morning fog

Fleabane

Providing for hungry pups requires adult coyotes to keep moving and hunting at a very busy pace.

This coyote was traveling diagonally towards me at a slow trot. She was alert to any sound in the grass that would indicate a rodent, chicks in a nest, or anything she might be able to eat. Any faint noise caused her to veer off in a different direction, or to stop, and as quietly as possible, to sneak up on things making noise in the grass. I could not hear the noises she heard, but it was clear she was hunting primarily by sound. I only needed to watch her ears as they swiveled and pointed to understand where she was concentrating. Sometimes she tipped her head sideways to help pinpoint a sound before making a pounce. If she was successful, she ate her catch, and if she missed, she wasted no time there but took off right away at a trot with her ears leading her on a zigzag course to find food for her pups.

Moving gently
toward me
through the
spring grass, this
garter snake had
little fear of me.

When photographing wildlife, it is
usually best to get to their eye level.
I can relate better to creatures if I can
look them in the eye. Twisting along,
it raised its head and looked intently at
my macro lens as I lay in the grass too.
Garter snakes eat earthworms, mice,
frogs, toads, and, occasionally, small fish.
I didn't look much like any of these,
so it slowly moved away, apparently
looking for something more its size.

Soaring on the rising
morning thermals
near Mammoth, this
red-tailed hawk was
taking its morning
catch to its nest.

Its catch was a small snake, probably a
garter snake. Redtails are North America's
most common buteo. Buteos are hawks
with broad rounded tails and wings
which allow them to soar high in slow,
wide circles. They float over large areas
hunting for rodents, rabbits, small birds,
and, occasionally, reptiles.

Herbivores find abundant food by mid-spring.
They have no trouble finding forbs, sedges, grasses, and leaves.

There are different ways of consuming this vegetation. The bull elk walked along with his nose at the ground to bite off what he liked. He chewed it a little, swallowed, and moved on looking for more.

The muskrat dove to the bottom of a pond and hauled up armloads of greens. He draped them over a secure log and, starting at one end of each tendril,

nibbled rapidly through dozens of pieces. I watched him consume ten armloads in about one hour, using his front feet to feed the greenery into his vegetable chopper.

The pika scurried over and around the rocks on a talus slope to get to small mats of forbs. There she bit off her favorites and, after she had enough for a mouthful, gathered them up and hopped back to

her secure shelter under a large boulder.

The baby marmot walked out away from the rocks to select a single grass stem. He bit it off close to the ground, carried it back to the edge of the rocks, and sat on his butt to eat it. He held the grass stem by one end in his dexterous front feet and twisted and pulled it toward himself as he ate.

A crab spider does not build a web, but instead waits in ambush on the edge of a flower.

The Lincoln's sparrow seasonally occupies virtually all of the North American continent.

It nests on the ground in the grasslands from Alaska south to central Nebraska and winters as far south as El Salvador. I found this little energetic omnivore carrying mouthfuls of mayflies to her nest in the grass below an old stump. She consistently landed on this tip of a branch to look around for predators before she dropped into the grass with food for her chicks. I didn't walk over to look at the nest for fear of creating a scent trail that might lead a coyote to the chicks later. Her predictable stop on the branch did provide me with an opportunity to set up and prefocus on her perch and to photograph a small busy bird, usually a difficult subject.

The spider's prey is the unwary fly or mosquito that has come to feed on the flower's nectar. The crab spider walks sideways and has front legs that are stronger than its hind legs, like the crustacean. When an insect lands on the spider's flower, the spider will steal up behind the insect, leap out, and stab it in the neck, paralyzing it. Injecting it with a dissolving enzyme, the spider consumes the insect's insides, then casts the empty husk aside.

Aspen grove in Round Prairie

Both adult red-naped sapsuckers were bringing beaks full of ants to their chicks in the nesting cavity of an aspen tree.

Landing at the opening, they looked around, then quickly disappeared into the hole causing a lot of cheeping sounds from the chicks who fought over the new load of ants. The adults reappeared head first and flew straight out of the hole. About every sixth visit, they left with a fecal sac, flying out from the tree about 15 yards to drop it before going on to look for more ants.

Wild strawberry

A showy perennial, the arrowleaf balsamroot has
a very long taproot and thrives on dry, rocky hillsides.

The large, velvety, sage-colored leaves are

shaped like arrowheads, and the cheerful

yellow blossoms could easily be mistaken

for sunflowers.

The wild iris is sometimes called blue flag.

It grows in damp ground. In full bloom, from a distance, dense stands of these flowers can look like a small light blue pond. The 2–3 inch long blossoms open their graceful petals in soaring wing-like arrays. The iris appears ready to flutter away like a butterfly.

Old Faithful

The soft light near sunrise is·usually the best light of the day for photography.

Traveling at an extremely low angle through the cool damp air, the light picks up soft warm tones of pink, magenta, and orange. If there are high clouds above, they reflect and scatter the color down over the whole landscape. Geysers, fog, and water all take on the color of the clouds.

Electric Peak
from Swan Lake

Hundreds of spider webs were strung at all angles between the cinquefoil bushes.

One corner of each web started at or near the top of a twig at about knee height. The webs were ready to seine the flood of insects that would warm up and appear about the same time the dew evaporated off the webs and left them nearly invisible again.

I like star track photographs because they illustrate
something that is absolutely real, though we
can't quite see it.

We can't sit and watch the movement of
the stars. We see them only in brief instants
as dots, not as tiny light streaks arcing
across the dark sky.

One afternoon in early June, I noticed a female pronghorn lying by herself.
This made me stop and look more closely at her....

Pronghorns are gregarious animals so, if one is by itself, there is something unusual happening. The individual could be sick, injured, or at this time of year, giving birth or caring for newborns. I looked at her very carefully and noted several things. She was still pregnant; her bag was tight and full of milk. While she was lying down, she did not chew her cud but squirmed and fidgeted. When she stood up, she was not interested in moving more than a few yards, and she did not appear to be hurt or sick.

I was raised and spent 20 years on a cattle ranch in western South Dakota where I learned more than I wanted to know about cows. Many of the things I learned then about animal behavior apply now in my work with wildlife. The outward signs of a pregnant Hereford cow, or of an elk, bison, pronghorn, or other ungulate preparing to give birth are nearly identical. All those thousands of hours I spent as a kid watching pregnant cows, pulling calves, and watching newborn calves and their anxious mothers taught me that this pronghorn doe was going to give birth in the next few hours.

A pronghorn's primary defense is its ability to run. If she felt nervous or threatened, she could run away faster than any other land animal on this continent,

but she tolerated my presence, so I settled down to watch her.

She was alert to everything around her, even to a red-tailed hawk floating high above us. After about one hour she got up and slowly walked past me and over a nearby hill. I picked up my equipment and followed her about a half a mile staying 100-200 yards from her. She stopped now and then to lie down. On a small, flat knoll, she stopped and lay down for about half an hour.

It had been two hours since I first saw her, and I started worrying that the sun would go down and I would lose my light before she gave birth. Occasionally she breathed rapidly for a few seconds then calmed down again. She stretched out on her side and stiffened up, then tucked her feet back under her and quietly waited.

Finally, when she was standing, two tiny feet appeared. She lay down and stretched out her legs and squirmed and pushed, breathing hard. The feet disappeared, then reappeared with a tiny nose. She stood up, then lay back down on her other side stretching out flat on the ground again.

She pushed and squirmed, lifted her head up over her back, and let out a whispered moan. The shiny wet head and shoulders of a fawn appeared.

Standing up, she sniffed and looked around for her new fawn. However, the fawn was dangling from its mother, like a thick wet towel, stuck at the hips....

On the ranch, I would occasionally have to catch a cow and tie a rope on the front legs of a calf and pull it free because it was stuck at the hips. The mother and fawn would both die if she was not able to complete the birth. Lying down again after a minute or so, the pronghorn stretched and pushed some more until the fawn was finally born. The doe stood up and smelled her new fawn and licked its face. The dark, wet gray fawn looked dead. Then it wiggled its head and started to breathe, trying to figure out which way was up. Mom licked the newborn's face until the fawn could keep its head up and breathe well.

I felt the same flood of wonder and awe at the sight of this tiny delicate pronghorn that I had felt years before when I watched a calf first breathe. I saw the same impulse in this trembling little pronghorn to move and struggle, and to stand up.

Meanwhile, mom was giving birth to another one. She lay down beside the first fawn and went through much of the same effort, except the second one slipped out all at once. They were born about five minutes apart and looked identical. While the second one was still trying to learn how to breathe, the first one was shivering with the effort to control all those tiny new muscles.

The first fawn shivered and raised its little butt slightly up off the ground, then dropped flat. Next, it tried to extend its front legs, which caused it to twist and tip over on its side....

It raised its rear end nearly all the way up, but this did not coordinate with any motion on its front end, and it flopped over in the dirt again.

Finally, it got its hind legs standing and was up on its knees, then the rear end wobbled back and forth and it fell down. Each time it tried something, it seemed to learn what worked and cumulatively all the right actions added up to the ability to stand.

When it did stand on all four legs for the first time, it took every bit of its concentration and strength. Waves of trembling went through it, and it fell down again. For the next couple of minutes it practiced standing up; each time it got up more quickly than the last. Its most stable posture was when its legs were sprawled out. Now that it could stand reasonably well, it wanted to walk. The first time it picked up one front foot to

move, it tipped over in that direction just as if it had fallen into a hole. The next time it picked up the same foot, but leaned back away from falling in that hole again, which caused it to tumble backwards the other way. As it wobbled and tried to learn how to operate its four legs, it pitched over backwards, or tipped onto its nose. It picked up one foot and raised it way too high to take a step so that the other three

legs collapsed. The second fawn by now had learned to stand and was also trying to learn to walk in the right direction; actually, any direction would have done if it could have just stayed upright.

One of my impulses was to go over and hold the little guys so they wouldn't fall down all the time and hurt themselves, but I knew that creatures have been going through this process for millions of years without my help, so any interference from me was undoubtedly not necessary.

At last, they were able to coordinate their legs and stay on their feet for more than 15 seconds at a time. One was able to skitter sideways for two or three feet and stay upright, and I could see a little more confidence and less trembling. For a while, they didn't know which direction their little bodies would go. It could be forward, back-

ward, sideways like a crab, or headfirst into the cactus. When they finally had a little control over their direction of travel, they started trying to walk to their mom. Staggering toward her, they stood a foot away from her and tried to reach out and nurse. They would go off balance and fall on their faces. When they stood up again, they usually faced the wrong direction and fell down trying to turn around.

They would start toward her, take four quick, wobbly steps, crash into her, and fall down. A dozen times each got just the right distance from her, but tried to nurse her neck or her knee....

The drive to stand up, to walk, and then to nurse consumed all their energy and attention. The mother stood patiently as they moved all around her trying to find her milk. When they finally stood in the right place, nuzzled around her bag and got hold of a nipple, they nursed for only about 20 seconds. That little bit of nourishment satisfied and completed their first elemental drive to live.

They wandered in a small area around their mother in curious amazement. Because the world was new to them, every sight, sound, and smell was enticing and benign. The mother still had a lot to worry about, because the newborns were totally helpless and couldn't even outrun a field mouse. She had chosen her birthing spot well. She could watch for predators from the small level spot below the ridgeline, and

a predator would have to get close before it could see the little fawns. She lay down to rest about an hour and a half after the twins were born, obviously tired.

The twins walked around for another ten minutes. When they had lain down too, I stood up carefully so I wouldn't startle them, and walked directly away and out of sight, thankful and exhilarated that I had witnessed the entire event and all were safe.

Ornithologists
split bird rearing
behavior into
two groups—
altricial and
precocial.

Altricial birds, such as robins, eagles, and
warblers are fed in the nest by the adults.
Adult precocial birds, on the other hand,
provide protection and warmth and take
their young to places where the chicks have
to figure out what is edible and collect it
themselves; examples are geese, plovers,
and grouse. An indication of altricial birds is
that the chicks hatch naked and helpless and
stay in the nest, whereas precocial birds
hatch covered with fuzzy down and are up
and running around in a matter of minutes.
This blue grouse hen was providing warmth
and protection here in the early morning
for her four precocial chicks. After watching
me for about ten minutes they all got up,
stretched, scratched, and wandered out
from under the spruce tree to feed.

Sandhill cranes nest
on the ground in
marshy, open areas.

Their nests are large mounds of grass and
reeds built up above the dampness of
the surrounding terrain. All adults have
blue-gray feathers but in the Yellowstone
region they soon become stained a rusty
brown from smearing iron rich mud and
water over themselves while preening.
This coloration turns out to be helpful by
providing great camouflage in the brown
mud and grass. When an adult lowers its
head and sits still on its nest, it becomes
nearly invisible.

A common member of the thrush family, the American robin can be seen in most of North America.

It eats earthworms, insects, and berries. In mid-June one year I came across this juvenile huddled on a low cottonwood branch. It was content to sit and wait for its mom to bring it insects. Its mom appeared about every five minutes with a beak full of food: spiders, mayflies, or a mashed-up bug of some type. The chick fluttered its wings and dropped its head down while pointing its open mouth toward mom. Quickly stuffing a beak full of food down junior's red throat, the adult would wait a few seconds to watch the chick swallow everything and then fly away to find more food. She came this time with a salmon fly, a large type of stone fly that lives all of its life under water except for its last few days when it emerges from the stream and flies around to locate other salmon flies, mate, lay eggs and then die. An orange salmon fly is up to three inches long, and this one was a difficult mouthful for the chick to eat. The chick was willing, but the insect kept sticking out all over the place; legs, wings, feet, and the orange abdomen would snag on the chick's beak as mom kept taking the giant insect back to reposition it. Finally mom got the salmon fly pointed head first down the chick's throat and watched as several slow swallows made it disappear.

Cutoff Mountain from lower Lamar Valley

This elk newborn had just learned to stand up.
The calf stood spraddle-legged and trembling...

in the cool morning air right beside its mother, who had decided to lie down. The calf was unable to nurse while the mother was lying down, so it nuzzled its mother's side and felt around in the determined instinctual way all newborn mammals have. Even though the cow was protective, solicitous, and tender, it didn't do the calf much good until she finally stood up. The calf continued to feel and nuzzle the mother's sides, knees, neck, and finally her nipples. The calf nursed and satisfied the third major drive it has, right after breathing and walking.

The thick evening haze appeared to be fog.
Strong backlighting from the setting sun created long shadows
and light streaks over the dark tree-lined ridges.

I expected it to become damp as the haze
moved my way. Then I noticed a faint
greenish yellow dust on my 500mm lens
hood. Rising from the stands of lodgepole
pine, the haze was pollen, silently floating

over Blacktail Plateau. Dispersing over
hundreds of square miles of lodgepole pines,
it was continuing the process of plant
regeneration which started hundreds of
millions of years ago.

An elk cow gives her calf a lot of attention for the first month or so.

She is in sight of it virtually all the time and occasionally rests right beside it. This calf was content to sleep most of the time, but looked up and sniffed at its mom's head when the cow scanned the nearby hillside for possible threats. Since there were no problems visible, the cow looked gently at her beautiful calf and started to chew her cud. Comforted, the calf soon went back to sleep.

Imprinting by tiny, golden goslings shows how attentive even the very young Canada geese are.

The little ones are rarely more than a few feet from an adult. They may be feeding on some grass, but if the parent steps away from the goslings' safe zone, the goslings will race to be closer to the adult and a safe spot. If one is sleeping on the grass, it is constantly opening one eye to see where the adults are and will immediately jump up and chase after an adult who has moved off too far.

Migrating Canda geese

Little nondescript house wrens add a great deal
of life and vigor to Yellowstone.

They are quick and busy zipping over and

through the grasses and bushes catching

insects, stopping briefly but often to look

around and sing. They choose sturdy nesting sites, generally cavities in trees. They don't make the cavities; they find existing holes with small openings and carry twigs, grasses, and soft nesting materials into these secure spots.

Mountain bluebirds are also cavity nesters.

These two mountain bluebird chicks were very curious about the bright new world they would soon inhabit. But first, where was lunch?

Hayden Valley

Uinta ground squirrels are common rodents in the dry meadows of northern Yellowstone.

Although they don't live in densely populated "towns" like prairie dogs, they do live in colonies. It is unusual to see more than two close together and rare to see seven of them clustered together. This group includes the mother in the middle and six of her nearly grown babies looking nervously around. They are nervous most of the time because nearly everything eats them. Raptors fall from the sky on them, coyotes and foxes run across the ground at them, and badgers and bears dig them out of their burrows.

Western tanager

Meanderings of
Beaverdam Creek

The moose is the
largest member of the
deer family.

A calf is born reddish-brown with no
spots. His ungainliness and floppy snout
give him a somewhat comical appearance.
I have watched young calves kneeling
to browse the green vegetation because
their necks appeared to be just a little too
short to reach the ground comfortably.

Swimming slowly back and forth across a small pond, this goldeneye hen was caring for eight ducklings.

She provided protection and took them to shallow places where there was plenty of food. Since she does not feed her precocial ducklings, they were each diving to the bottom to find food. The ducklings' light fluffy down kept them warm and buoyant but made it difficult for them to stay under-water. They jumped up into the air to get a run at their dives and, when they came back up through the surface of the water, they popped up like ping pong balls.

Late afternoon,
Yellowstone Lake

In the spring cow elk are more attentive to danger than at any other time
of year because of their concern for the safety of their calves.

As the herd drifted around near Obsidian Creek, grazing the green grass in the fresh snow, two mature cows stood shoulder to shoulder and kept watch over the group. They watched the calves running through the group playing tag, seemingly unaffected by the influence of gravity. Threats to their calves could appear at any time from the surrounding lodgepole forest or from the hidden grassy edge of the creek. In order to maintain a constant assessment of all this activity and terrain, they had to keep turning their heads back and forth in all directions.

(previous pages)
Two young bison
calves sparring

In May of 2002, I had the good fortune to spend four days with a female grizzly bear and her two cubs along Obsidian Creek.

She was referred to as number 264 by the Interagency Bear Team which monitors the grizzlies of the Greater Yellowstone Ecosystem. She spent nearly all her life near the road corridor from Swan Lake Flat to Norris. The theory about this unusual preference of hers to stay near the road is that it was safer there from large males who are afraid of the road, and consequently, it is also underutilized bear habitat. She learned that humans were not a threat to her, so she lived unconcerned with the crowds of people excitedly watching her. Unfortunately, one of the hazards of this behavior is the possibility of getting hit by a car. For twelve years she survived traffic, but in June 2003 she was killed by an automobile. In the spring of 2002 she had successfully raised two cubs, and all three were feeding on a winter-killed bison cow within 100 yards of the road. This predictable food source allowed me the rare opportunity to return each day and spend hours watching them go about their daily lives. They were feeding, play-fighting, nursing, scratching, burying and uncovering the bison carcass, chasing ravens and coyotes, daydreaming, and playing keep-away with a chunk of elk hide.

Grizzly bears are intelligent animals; they can be very playful when they are well fed and feel secure.

These two bears, mom and one of her two cubs, had fed on a bison carcass and wandered around on the creek bottom, stopping to scratch and roll in the fresh snow. Mom sat in the snow and grass absentmindedly scratching, then reached down, picked up one of her hind feet, and played with her toes. She leaned back and did a reverse somersault. After rolling around some more she sat up again facing the other direction and played with the toes of her other hind foot. Meanwhile her cub had found a small stick. He chewed on it and rolled it around on his chest while lying on his back. After he accidentally dropped it, he raised his front legs up in the air, either looking for the stick or stretching.

Bison calves, like all infants, spend significant time playing.

Playing develops strength, coordination and agility as well as bonding and competitiveness as a calf seeks a place in the herd's hierarchy. This cow and calf were unusual because they played together for about five minutes. I have rarely seen cows play with their calves for more than 30 seconds.

The cow stood with her head down, encouraging the calf to push against her. The calf backed up with her tail in the air and made short runs at her mom's head. The calf danced around thumping into the cow's large skull but could not move it even an inch.

There was very little light in the timber where this great gray owl was spending the day.

It was perched about 25 feet off the ground. To get an eye level angle, I climbed up a small nearby ridge and set up my 500mm lens with a 1.4 teleconverter. The fastest exposure I could get was one-eighth of a second. To minimize camera movement, I locked the mirror up and fired the shutter with an electronic release. All this fussing around and all the unusual noises I made caused the owl to consider me a very curious creature indeed.

Morning fog near the mouth of Alum Creek

Male pollen cones of lodgepole pine

Tree swallows are cavity nesters, which means they nest in holes in wood.

This is an adult looking out from her nest site in the trunk of a dead aspen tree. She watched me for a minute or so with her bright shiny eyes, then pulled back into the shadow of her hole and folded up there in the dark to sit on her tiny white eggs in a feather lined cup.

While walking through a thicket of young lodgepole pine, I found this mule deer fawn....

The fawn was holding very still, hoping I would not see it. I set up a big telephoto lens and moved back and forth slightly to position the fawn's head between the green branches. As I stood in one spot, it continued to be a statue. After five or six minutes, it relaxed, looked around its immediate vicinity, lay down, and nearly disappeared from my sight behind the pine boughs.

Hillside near Mammoth shaped by Pinedale glaciers

An itch can be caused by many things and the contortions mammals go through to relieve those itches vary widely.

The bull elk was trying to direct his new, long antler tip to a small spot on his lower left flank. His antlers had been growing rapidly over the past month, and he didn't know exactly where they ended.

The moose licked its belly, but for some reason had to do it on three legs. For a brief time the moose glanced back at me under its leg before going back to grazing.

The bison calf gave the base of his jaw a couple of quick hard scratches with his hind foot. He got rid of what was bothering him and went right back to grazing.

The pronghorn fawns were lying on an anthill, and the large black ants crawled all over them, upset at the fawns' choice of resting spots. Wiggling their ears and rubbing their heads in the grass, the fawns tried

to get rid of the ants. One tried to scratch with its left rear leg while lying down, but couldn't keep up with the tickling, biting, moving ants, so the fawn stood up and scratched the top of his head and neck. Then it squirmed and stomped the ground, and lay back down on the anthill again because it was supposed to stay there, invisible in the grass, where its mom had left it.

A half dozen elk cows and two young calves were resting and grazing in the rich spring grass near Mammoth.

There was a small flock of cowbirds feeding in the grass between the elks' legs. The birds occasionally flew up and landed on the elks' backs. Seven birds lined up on one cow's back. The cow continued grazing and ignored them. Soon, though, the birds were hopping around arguing about their favorite spot on the thick hairy carpet, and the males were doing their mating display. After a couple minutes of these shenanigans, the cow stopped grazing, turned her head around, and looked down her back at the black chorus line. She could have said, "Look guys, cool it! This isn't a dance floor!" She returned to her grazing and, after a short while, the birds flew off one by one.

White pelicans are common in the spring and summer on Yellowstone's larger lakes.

They nest on the Molly Islands on Yellowstone Lake and feed in the large slow moving rivers of the Yellowstone plateau. Breeding adults have a fibrous plate on the upper mandible which is shed after the eggs are laid. They feed in flocks by herding fish into shallow water. Stabbing their beaks after the fish, they catch them in their gular pouch, which hangs below the lower mandible, let the water drain out, and swallow them whole.

Angel Terrace

A flock of about 200 cliff swallows were perching in this dead pine tree. The flock settled down all over the branches...

on the top half of the tree, 25-50 feet off the ground. In a group of this size, someone was bound to be bickering with someone else, so there were always a half dozen birds in midair, usually pushed off a branch by more aggressive neighbors. The loser of an argument flew around looking for an open spot to land and either landed and forced one of the others off or was rejected and had to continue flying. There was a steady flutter of wings scattered through the group as individuals rearranged themselves on branches or dropped off one branch and flew to another. For no reason I could see, about every five minutes the entire flock would explode off the tree and rise upward like dry leaves in a whirlwind. They scattered and disappeared, but, within a minute they came back, a dozen at first; then a hundred circled the tree and filled up the branches again.

Yellowstone's air is almost always pure and dry.

The high Yellowstone plateau has little dust in the air, yet it is cool or even cold at night in the spring so the humidity stays low. Light often stays clear and neutral colored throughout the day. The quality of the light varies but maintains a clarity that is rare in our industrialized world. When there is smoke in the air from a forest fire we see saturated oranges in the sky, yet usually the overall sense is that the air is clean. Color seems to glow from the clouds. The moon is usually a clean white in the sky near richly colored clouds. Reflections of a crystal blue sky are saturated and enhanced by the stillness and purity of the Yellowstone River's quiet surface. The thin wispy cirrus clouds at sunset glow with color from a prismatic effect on the high, icy moisture. Rainbow colors appear at the edge of these clouds.

Yellowstone River above
LeHardy Rapids

The male mountain
bluebird wears some
of the richest blue
colors found on a
North American bird.

Intense colors like these seem counter-
productive for his survival. He stands out
in contrast to everything in Yellowstone
as he buoyantly flies above the grassy
meadows he inhabits. This adult male
was watching over the surrounding area
while resting between feeding sessions.
The female and he methodically carried
insects to noisy chicks in a nearby nest.

(previous pages)
Goblinland at night

East face of Electric Peak

Cool morning mists, Lamar Valley

There are plenty of hazards for young calves, so it is important for them to obey their mothers implicitly.

When a cow wants her calf to move, it is impressive to see how a calf will thrash and struggle through thick brush and water, go up steep muddy hills, and hurry along in the straightest line to stay close. They usually don't look at what they have to go through; they just stay right near mom.

They usually don't even try to go around anything: "If mom just went there, I must too." The calf waits right next to mom when she stops to look around. The very young calves usually have no idea why they are in such a hurry, but they follow along with blind determination.

There are several bull elk that spend the spring and summer along Cascade Creek.

They graze the open grassy parks on the 8000-foot-high Yellowstone plateau. They can be found in the early morning lying down, chewing their cud, and watching the fog empty out of the trees. Before the dew evaporates from the grass, they get up, stretch, scratch, and yawn, in preparation for another easy day of spring living.

Wood grain with lichen

I like the way fog isolates elements of a landscape...

usually by obscuring distractions in the distance. Interesting things happen graphically at the edge of fog. A single little tree on a hummock can be made into a strong part of a composition because the complex forest in the distance is softened and minimized by fog.

Close inspection of even a dead lodgepole pine can reveal beautiful abstract shapes and textures.

This was one of millions of pine trees killed by the North Fork fire in 1988. The fire did not consume most of the trees; instead it burned the needles and scorched the bark, leaving the majority of the trees intact and standing, but dead. As the bark dried, it shrank, cracked, curled up, and eventually fell off. The process of shedding the bark can take years, so a stand of trees can occupy someone like me, with a macro lens, for hours, looking for abstract shapes in the metamorphosis of bark and the revelations of the insect activity that occurred under the bark.

Great gray owls nest in heavy timber near green, grassy meadows.

Minimal effort seems to be given to nest construction. They will take over an old raven's nest or use a natural feature as shown here. This lodgepole pine had broken off about 15 feet above the ground. When the forest fires of 1988 burned through here, the fire charred the bark and burned down into the top of the stump, creating a perfectly symmetrical six-inch-deep bowl. The three owlets watched me curiously as I walked all around them. When I saw them lined up with the two large splinters of wood on either side, I made this photograph, and left, so their mother would come back soon.

Clearing fog after three days of rain

Lower Falls, late afternoon

Lichen is a combination of fungus and algae.

It is found in all life zones, even the dry plains of Antarctica, and is most readily noticed in Yellowstone on exposed rock surfaces. Often different colonies of lichens will completely cover a rock's surface in an abstract multicolored mosaic. They often grow outward from a point in an expanding disc or oval shape. Gray is a common color, but they can also be rich reds, yellows, blues, and oranges.

Black billed magpies belong to the same family as jays, crows, ravens, and European jackdaws. This family of birds is notoriously noisy, aggressive, and smart. The magpie is probably the smartest of them all. The iridescent black wings and graceful long tail will shine green, blue, or silvery in different light. I have often had one of these birds land on a nearby branch and squeak, chirp, whistle, purr, and squawk, look me in the eye, and tell me the story for the day. I usually say something back to it, but we don't seem to understand each other, and I, at least, feel I've missed something important.

An elk cow will tolerate a lot of a magpie's investigations.

While this cow was lying in the grass chewing her cud, the magpie walked nearby, looking for bugs and worms in the grass. He wandered along until he ended up beside the cow's feet. He bent down, looked sideways at the cow's left rear hoof, and gently pecked between her toes. I couldn't see what he was after, but he tapped several times on both of her hind feet. The cow looked briefly at the bird, wiggled her ears, and ignored him. Calling aack, aack, aack, the magpie hopped up on the cow's belly and walked to the high point of her back. He looked all around from this fuzzy perch, while the cow still ignored him, not even seeming to notice when he flew off to the trees.

Lodgepole pine on island
in Yellowstone River

Base of Specimen Ridge above
flooding Lamar River

Standing on long thin legs, sandhill cranes are between three and four feet tall.

A fossil humerus bone found in nine-million-year-old Miocene deposits in Nebraska is identical to those of modern sandhill cranes. These majestic prehistoric birds have watched several continental glaciers advance and retreat. They were an ancient species before many of Yellowstone's features appeared. Calling with a rattling, musical gar--oo--oo, they can be heard up to a mile away. With only about 60 nesting pairs in Yellowstone, it can be difficult to see them. At first glance I have mistaken the rusty colored cranes, feeding with their heads down, as deer. Sandhills are omnivorous, eating worms, seeds, roots, insects, and small rodents.

Upper end of the Black Canyon
of the Yellowstone

The American black bear can be black, brown, or even white.

This little cub was one of a pair of cinnamon-colored twins from a black mom. These cubs had the phenomenal energy of healthy infants and attention spans of about three nano-seconds. They raced around through the tall grass and flowers, bit twigs, swatted at the butterflies, wrestled a two-foot tall pine tree almost to the ground, and then climbed up the fat trunk of a giant fir tree like sticky monkeys. About 30 feet up the tree this cub walked out as far as he dared on a springy green branch until it bent and quivered under his meager weight, the soft green needles hiding him and brushing his golden hair. He squirmed and stretched and then turned around on his precarious yielding perch and made it back to the relative safety of the two-foot diameter trunk. Looking around the trunk, he appeared to be checking to see if there were any more adventures to be had on the opposite side.

One day old pronghorn fawn

Sleeping pronghorn fawn

I was busy photo-
graphing some early
springbeauty blossoms
in a damp area on
the north side of
Sulphur Mountain....

The Mary Mountain bison herd, which
numbers over 1000 head, lives in this area.
I could see several hundred of them in the
sage covered grasslands to the north of me.
I was concentrating, down on my knees,
and thrashing around with a tripod in the
mud. Apparently this kind of bizarre
behavior intrigued one of the young bison
calves. He walked slowly toward me, stopping once in a while to look back to see if
the rest of his relatives found my behavior
as odd as he did. He was the only one who
had the curiosity or nerve to want a closer
inspection. After I saw him coming, I put
on a long lens and stayed low on my knees
to see what he would do. He came as close
as he dared. He twisted his head around
and peeked through the sage, sniffing.
Finally he decided I wasn't worth any
more effort or risk to get closer. He turned
and walked away, then kicked up his heels
and ran back to the others.

Spring is the most
extreme season.

In the midst of an abundance of
birth and revitalization there are large
numbers of creatures that will die.
A natural system, like Yellowstone's,
uses these deaths to sustain itself. Just
as this bull elk took from the earth
to support himself, his body will
now settle back into the earth and
nourish others.

Blacktail Plateau,
evening shower

Wind patterns on Yellowstone Lake
near Steamboat Point

Clouds are one of the
most dynamic and
ephemeral features of
our landscape.

They weigh thousands of tons, but float
gracefully across the sky. Sometimes they
are nearly featureless looming gray masses
and sometimes their fantastic colors will
even distract us from a field of wildflowers.
The sun backlit the outline of this cloud
and appeared as a small gold sliver along
the top.

Built from rough blocks of
columnar basalt, quarried
near the water tower in
Gardiner, Montana...

the Roosevelt Arch was dedicated by
President Theodore Roosevelt in April
1903 and finished shortly thereafter. For
100 years it has stood and welcomed the
world to the first national park and to one
of the finest areas of wild land remaining
on this continent. The arch with the rich
rainbow glowing beyond the glistening
wet rock, symbolizes for me that a paradise still awaits visitors in Yellowstone.

TOM MURPHY

Tom Murphy's photographic passion and specialty is Yellowstone Park. Since 1975 he has traveled extensively within its 3400 square miles, hiking thousands of miles and skiing on dozens of extended overnight trips in the backcountry. He has skied across the park twice, once on a 14-day solo trip. Two things motivate him to travel carrying a heavy backpack: a desire to see Yellowstone's wilderness backcountry and to photograph the behaviors of free-roaming wildlife and the colors, shapes, and textures of the land.

His photographs have been used, both editorially and commercially, in numerous regional, national, and international publications. Clients include: *Life, Architectural Digest, National Geographic, Audubon* and *Time. Newsweek, The New York Times Magazine, National Geographic Adventure, Esquire,* and others have sent him on assignments.

His first book, *Silence and Solitude, Yellowstone's Winter Wilderness,* won a 2002 Montana Book Award. The video, *Silence and Solitude,* produced by Montana Public Television, earned an Emmy nomination for Tom's photography.

He donates the use of his photographs to environmental groups, supporting their efforts to preserve wildlife and wild land. In 1984 he graduated with honors from Montana State University with a Bachelor of Science in Anthropology. He lends his backcountry skills to the Park County Search and Rescue team, which he helped to organize 20 years ago. He was the first person licensed to lead photography tours in Yellowstone Park and operates, with his wife Bonnie, Wilderness Photography Expeditions. He also teaches workshops and special seminars for camera clubs, nature centers, and institutions such as the Yellowstone Association and Montana State University.

WILDLIFE PHOTOGRAPHY ETHICS

Good wildlife photography ethics assume that all creatures have a right to go about their lives without interference from us. The best wildlife photographs illustrate what an animal's life is like. How does it make its living? How does it interact with its environment? How does it respond to others of its own species and to different species? How does it play? What are its feeding, traveling, resting, and other behaviors like? If a photographer disrupts an animal's actions, not only is he distracting and modifying the animal's life and potentially causing it harm, he is not going to photograph natural behavior. I am not interested in photographing an animal's response to me. I want to show the beauty and uniqueness of a creature's daily life.

To avoid disturbing an animal's daily routine, it is best to use long telephoto lenses. An automobile is one of the best blinds from which to photograph in national parks. You must observe and understand wildlife's behaviors. Learn to read their body language and if your presence is disturbing them, even 300 yards away, leave at once. I think of myself as a visitor in their living room and try to be a humble and considerate guest.

ACKNOWLEDGEMENTS

A sincere thank you is always necessary for any successful project.
Thank you to Bonnie for her continued support, help, and encouragement.
To Netzy Durfey, Janet Bailey, Edie Linneweber, and Anne Norberg for help typing and proofreading.
To Dave Long for careful attention to the high quality scans he made of these photographs.
To Adrienne Pollard for her wonderful work assembling and presenting 25 years of my spring images in this book.
To the wild lands of Yellowstone and to the innocent beauty of all the creatures who live there.